SMARTYpants
secrets

Gently
AGING

Going Through the Inevitable Process with Health, Fun, and Frolic!

D.R. Martin, PhD*
(*Personal human Development)

SmartyPants Press
Falmouth, Maine 04105
www.SmartyPantsSecrets.com

ISBN 13: 978-1-943971-16-9
   10: 1943971161

Copyright 2016 D.R. Martin, PhD*
(*Personal human Development)

The SmartyPants Secrets Concept

A **SmartyPants Secret** is that **one piece of information** that you need to know to make every job a little bit, or maybe a lot, **easier**. Almost everything we do in life has a SmartyPants secret that to it, that knowing the "secret" would help tremendously in shortening the learning curve.

After experiencing many "a ha!" moments that were previous head bangers, I realized that there was a lot of grief – i.e. aggravation, wasted time, spent resources - that could have been saved if I had known to tap into the insider information that others had and I was lacking. A SmartyPants secret is that crucial bit of timely knowledge.

We all want a magic bullet answer that solves all of our problems in one fell swoop and makes everything go perfectly well, preferably in record time! We want that magic to happen right NOW, to be easily done, and to be preferably cheap, or at least not at great expense. There are a lot of demands on our unattainable magic ☺

For example, one day I looked at my face and damn if I didn't see a "sun spot" (nastily also called a "liver" spot) marring the surface of my otherwise smooth face on the right lower cheek. I scheduled an appointment at the dermatologist to verify the find and see if it could be lasered off. She sent me to an aesthetician who gave me some key information that made a huge difference in my decision of what to do next.

I was told that my even slightly darker (Asian) skin carries more pigment than Caucasian skin obviously. But what's not obvious is the way the body works, specifically the way the skin works, which is that when you wound the skin's surface, which laser surgery would certainly do, extra pigments rush to the spot to heal it (the "job" of pigment is to protect the underlying cells). The net result is that non-Caucasian skin heals into darker scabs and scars. (I have noticed this phenomena before but never made a direct connection.) Why then would I ever choose to have laser surgery on my face to remove a mark only to end up with an even darker mark? Yikes!

Obviously I wouldn't, but without this specialized knowledge about different results with different skin types, that even the dermatologist didn't know (yes, she was the recommender of the laser surgery option) I would've made a poor decision, with permanent negative results. A SmartyPants timely secret to the rescue!

Experts, who have hours of experience doing what the newbie is attempting to do, have expert knowledge, which may not be so secret, but it is **key information** that the novice greatly needs.

If you've ever struggled with something then learned the 'something' afterwards that caused you to say to yourself or to say aloud, "*Well, **if I only known THAT before I did this**, it would've made a world of difference!*" then you just learned a SmartyPants secret - the hard way.

The short SmartyPants Secrets books give you the secret that you need on a given topic, the most important piece of information that makes the greatest difference between easier success and hard-fought failure.

When I was young there was a professor at Cornell University, which in his obituary listed him as "***the last man to know everything***." I was taken by the concept of anyone knowing everything there is to know contained in one brain. Oh, to have such a mind!

But **to know everything**, logical facts and figures, and **to be able to do everything** are **two different things**. Brain power doesn't equal skill and expertise.

Today that one brain that knows everything is the Internet. There is so much information today available on the Internet; we can all be like that professor at Cornell and have access to all knowledge at the click of our fingertips.

More knowledge than we could ever consume - **who has time** to go through it all? Most of the time **what you really want is to know is the crux of the subject** on hand, not the whole litany of everything imaginable that is available to know.

Tell me just what I need to know! (and I likely don't know what specific knowledge to ask for). It's literally impossible to know what you don't know. Let the expertise of knowledgeable others guide you.

If you are new to a topic the **SmartyPants secret can save you time and effort**, which are important to your success. Not a complete course on the topic, which you can certainly get elsewhere, the SmartyPants secrets concept is primarily to help you **not miss the key information needed for success**.

The building block of knowledge that the foundation rests upon; the Keystone or cornerstone knowledge makes a critical difference, especially when that knowledge that you do have, or think you have, is **faulty, incomplete or missing** entirely.

The concept of **social proof** states that when we have no prior experience in a given situation we rely on **others to show us the way**. We believe that lacking personal knowledge, that their situation is similar to our situation, and therefore what worked for them has a high probability of working for us.

We quiz others about our shared circumstances around the situation to verify that their solution is a good one. Plus, we think: *there's nothing to lose in trying since I don't have a better answer*.

Then when what worked for another doesn't happen to work for us, we are reminded that **we are all different people**, with different variables that impact success or failure. Some solutions to problems are hit or miss depending on who we are. And sometimes success depends on having and following the right key knowledge.

Solving problems is not the complete SmartyPants concept, although SmartyPants secrets can indeed offer real help for real problems. Rather the full concept is that having that key knowledge piece makes efforts easier and successful quicker; hopefully **avoiding having the problem in the first place**. We do anything in life because we have a goal to achieve. Reaching that goal successfully, quickly and easier than without knowing the SmartPants secret is the SmartyPants concept.

And because **all SmartyPants secrets have a physiological root**, grounded in our shared human biology, every SmartyPants secret is valid for everyone, no matter who you are. While we are all uniquely different from each other, we have a **common biology** consisting of inherited traits that stretch back to the Neanderthal era.

Applying a SmartyPants secret **will work for you no matter who you are**. And in our busy world, who doesn't want to save time and know the SmartyPants secret to anything?

Why ever risk hindering easier success by not knowing the core success secret?

Healthy, Gentle

AGING

We all must face the fact - Some with gritted teeth Some with real enjoyment All with a diminishment of physical abilities

I am 60. No, let's be truthful, I am 61, having had a birthday just a few days ago. All my high school and college friends are also 61, as is my husband of 41 years. I have some younger friends, none younger than 40 (who I realistically call 'friend', and not merely an 'acquaintance'), and several older friends, some up into their 80s. So I have seen this aging business, upfront and personal, for several decades now. And being the SmartyPants that I am, I've thought about this subject, asked lots of questions, and recorded the unique process that is different for every person (depending on diet, experience, individual makeup, etc.) but also has some similarities for all.

Obviously the focus in this book will be on the similarities we all experience, to set the younger reader's expectations who may be coming into the process, of what can be commonly expected as one slides gently into the 3rd stage of adulthood. Additionally useful, if there still is time in your horizon, are ideas about what you still might be able to do to lessen the 'ravages of time', if you so choose.

Attitudes on Aging Are Cultural

Different cultures view the aged among them with different levels of respect and value. Many are treated as venerable and wise due to their advanced years, and respect for their abilities. They need younger generations to take care of them, just as when it was their turn they did the same for their elders.

But what was old, and how long did this 'taking care of' go on for? In late medieval times, you were considered old if you lived past the age of 30 :(In early modern England the life expectancy for males was 33, for females it was 40 (so an overall average of 36 short years of life expectancy). With modern medical advances, of course, we think of people in their 30s as quite young. To die under the age of 40 is a life cut short, not a full life lived! But on the other end of the spectrum, for those who need to care for others with twice that lifespan can be a hardship that we're not equipped for, mentally or financially.

The United States has a history of independence, stronger than interdependence. We revere those who build their futures from scratch, who pull themselves up by their bootstraps, who become great successes due to hard work and much effort. By God, they have character! Clearly, we value productivity and culturally reward those who parlay that productivity with riches and great admiration.

We value our young so much in the U.S. that our culture revolves around standards of youth and beauty as the most important reflections of fertility and productivity. It's no wonder that so many of us push back against the greying and the wrinkles that signal a loss of both. (Not you? Ha! You wouldn't be reading this book if that were true.)

The flip side of that coin is that the elderly who are no longer productive in a meaningful way are cast aside by the younger capable generation. Being largely regarded as useless by a society that values utility, and then being mentally and physically discarded (tucked away in nursing homes which are seldom visited). This is not a wholly unexpected by-product of American misplaced values, even as we flinch against realizing the reality. Out of sight out of mind; no need to expose ourselves now to the nasty view of what our elderly futures may end up looking like.

When people were not expected to live much beyond their physically useful years anyway, this was not a problem. A largely agricultural society up to the 1900s, people toiled on farms, which was a hard physical life. The average life expectancy then was 47. By 1950 farms work was on the decline; factory jobs made working physically much easier. Life expectancy in 1950 had risen to 68 years.

By 2012 average US life expectancy was up to 78.8 years, peaking for women at 81.2 years. Today average life expectancy is 79.26 years, with women expected to outlive men by about 4.8 years (the why of which will be discussed in greater detail further on).

Many factors beyond physical job conditions impact life expectancy including race, gender, economics, hereditary health, and personal attributes, like diet, sleep patterns, alcohol and tobacco use, exercise, etc. plus where you choose to live; living location is a factor in determining how long you will live.

With industrialized nations life expectancy is higher than in developing nations due to better living conditions, and primarily impacted by availability to medical resources including advanced research and development.

The United States does not boast the best longevity of the developed nations (that honor goes to Japan and Switzerland), but it does hold the highest health spending title (with an eye to pricing of drugs and medical services as a large consideration factor).

The US does have the dubious boast of the highest obesity rate in the world, which clearly is a negative factor correlating with mortality. There can be too much of a good thing when it comes to an overabundance of food coupled with a culture rooted in cheering an independent attitude. ("Don't tell me what I can and cannot eat!")

The Baby Boomers – the generation born approximately between the years of 1946 to 1964 – were the largest generation seen in decades, due to all the jubilant soldiers returning home from World War II to young brides. This group, because of the ambience of the country during their growing up years, are today lamenting their lost youth and are fighting the aging process like no other generation.

The Baby Boomers, currently 52-70 years old, are our future senior citizens, even as they rebuke the label and fight the image of themselves as part of the elderly set ("Who ME - ask for seniors citizens discount?? Nahhh!")

Aging Changes Creep Up Ever So Slowly, but Steadily

You're going through life as you always have, then one day you realize that things just aren't the same as they used to be… you wonder, Hey, what gives? with your usually so consistently and dependably reliable body. You hate to slow down and admit that the aging process has started to rear its ugly head. And really, what choice do you have but to carry on and make moderate mental adjustments to accommodate the inevitable aging process.

I used to be able to push myself hard, staying up all night to finish a project, and bouncing right back with nary a notice.

I used to be able to fall asleep at the drop of a hat, stay asleep soundly for up to 16 hours as needed, if my body was recuperating from pending illness or lack of sleep the night before (that all night project).

I used to be able to eat whatever I wanted, whenever I wanted; sometimes barely eating for days during extreme focus periods, other times packing in 1000s of calories in a few short hours.

Then I turned 55, my "Hey, what gives?" year of noticing that things were not as they always were for decades before – recognition that the cursed aging process could not be denied.

Now when I stay up too late, still working on a project, I pay for it with waning stamina, lack of sustained focus (just not as sharp in the 16th hour as in the earlier hours), and a pressing need to recharge the batteries immediately, not days later.

Now sleep doesn't come as easily, both falling asleep and staying asleep are more difficult, making that restorative rest to rebuild the body choppy and inconsistent.

Now when I don't eat on a regular schedule, in regular amounts my system lets me know that all is not good, with regular heartburn, gas, and general G.I. track symptoms of discomfort. And when I eat too much junk food/wrong food, all kinds of stomach screaming lets me know that my onion ring days are limited if not altogether over. My father used to say, "I love cabbage, but it doesn't love me anymore" and my young self simply had no idea what he was talking about!

A word on heartburn, also called GERD (gastroesophageal reflux disorder) – beyond just an annoyance, it's a *disease* in later life.

Yes, my infrequent heartburn turned into a frequent occurrence in my late 50s, resulting in voice changes from a long enflamed esophagus, before I properly addressed the issue. It took years to clear, with the real potential of esophageal cancer had I continued to ignore this condition.

With age, each of the 5 senses decrease in sharpness (dare I say, "dull") for all, hearing and vision loss are the most troubling and impactful to both the quality and length of life.

Aging changes can make communication hard (what did you say?), decrease the enjoyment of certain activities (I just can't see as well as I used to), and strain interaction with others. It is well worth considering how to slow down or mitigate some of the aging process changes where possible, as life style choices can slow or speed up the coming age-related changes.

Dylan Thomas' Famous Poem

Do not go gentle into that good night
Old age should burn and rave at close of day
Rage, rage against the dying of the light

While written to describe death, this could easily be modified to describe the fight against the aging process, the death of youth:

Do not go gentle into the aging process
Youth should burn and rage at close of day
Rage, rage against the dying of your youth

Maybe not for all, but a worthy anthem for all of us Baby Boomers cringing at the thought of losing our vitality with continually diminishing abilities.

12 Aging Changes to Prepare for

Weight/Metabolism

Metabolism/bowels slow, with an ave 15 lb menopausal weight gain

- Men gain weight until around age 55, then start to lose it as testosterone levels drop

- Women gain weight until about age 65, and begin to lose it due to muscle tissue loss

- Medication dosages should be adjusted with aging body changes (less water, fat layer absorption)

- Muscle and tissue loss reduces the amount of water in the body, with greater dehydration potential

- Diet sensitivities develop with digestion processing changes; a slower metabolism doesn't work as quickly or as efficiently

- Reduced activity requires fewer calories

Gentle Aging Healthy Idea: *regular exercise plus eating several small "uniform" meals/day are easy to digest*

The Pull of GRAVITY

Changes in body shape with aging

- The amount and distribution of the body's basic building materials – fat, muscles, organs, bones, fluids – change with age.

- Fat tissue moves towards the body's center, the abdominal organs, and can increase up to 30%

- Lean body mass (muscles, organs) decreases

- Bones, muscles, and joints age, resulting in a loss of height after age 40 of .4 inches every 10 years; more after age 70.

- The heart, under pressure, thickens making it harder to maintain stamina, climbing stairs, etc. Keeping an eye on blood pressure is important to prolong healthy heart function.

- Feet become wider, from years of carrying the body's weight

Gentle Aging Healthy Idea: *changes can be offset by physical activity, diet, reducing stress, treating osteoporosis*

BALANCE Issues

Hearing is tied to balance, inner ear equilibrium

- Trying to move through time and space the same as before, only with diminished agility, results in misjudging distance and own speed of movement, resulting in bumping into things

- Lots of leg muscle mass and body shape changes affects balance, leading to falls

- Muscle weakness contributes to balance issues, corrected with strength building exercising

- Feet issues (bunions, hammer toes) affect gait and overall comfort with walking

- Years of improper footwear (ill-fitting or high heels) takes a toil, in foot, back, and leg issues

- Taking more than 4 prescriptions at once usually results in dizziness as a side effect

Gentle Aging Healthy Idea: *avoid the use of bath oils, scatter rugs, unstable footwear, which can cause slips and falls.*

SLEEP Patterns Zzzz...

Sleep is the body's restorative mechanism; an aging body has to repair and recharge, which is only possible with proper amounts of regular sleep

- Lower activity levels needs less calories consumption, and less sleep needed

- Broken sleep hurts cognitive function, which works best with continuous sleep

- Falling asleep issues include: sleep apnea, side effects of medications, bladder issues

- Older people need more, not less sleep, to repair and restore an aging body. A total of 8 1/2 hours for those over 60-70, 9 hrs for those over 70, including a daytime nap.

Gentle Aging Healthy Idea: *moderate exercise, not too close to bedtime, plus lowering the bedroom temperature helps with sleeping*

HEARING

Hearing becomes less sharp around age 50, impacting the quality of life, limiting interactions and communication with others, which can lead to isolation and loneliness

- Age causes certain ear mechanism parts to lose some of their functioning ability

- High pitched sounds are not heard well, if at all

- Ear wax becomes drier and more likely to cause blockage, reducing hearing ability

- 30% of those over 65 years old have significant hearing loss

Gentle Aging Healthy Idea: *proactively wearing earplugs and protective headgear during loud activities can help slow/prevent the decline; hearing aids after. Regular use of ear drops before the wax dries into a hard mass can save much pain later during professional wax removal and also improve hearing.*

VISION/Eyes

Vision, the sense we value the most, experiences major changes with age.

- Older eyes produce fewer tears, resulting in dry eyes, leading to cornea damage

- The pupil loses easy opening/closing function, making it harder to transition between bright light and darkness.

- Lenses lose their flexibility, eye muscles lose their tone → need for reading glasses

- Lenses yellow over time, making it harder to read yellow print, or low contrast colors on a yellow background.

- Retinal nerve cells die off, making it hard to see fine details

- Various common age-related vision conditions and diseases including cataracts, glaucoma, and macro degeneration – resulting in potential safety issues.

Gentle Aging Healthy Idea: *wear UV light-blocking sunglasses whenever out in bright sunlight; include dark leafy greens in healthy diet for vitamins and minerals.*

FLEXIBILITY Diminishes

Joints stiffen and muscles lose density, becoming less flexible.

- Muscle tone that is lost is harder to replace

- Bone density is lost causing posture changes

- Spinal vertebrae can be compressed, making the trunk look shorter and curved

- Hip and knee joints loose cartilage

- Finger joints and bones thicken slightly (especially in women)

- Finger sensitivity and dexterity reduction (pushing cell phone buttons)

Gentle Aging Healthy Idea: *exercise* – *yoga, Pilates, tai chi - can slow or prevent bone and muscle loss, help with balance, stretching maintains hips and knees; nutrition (calcium, vitamin D) for maintaining strength, balance, flexibility. Muscles need to be stretched! Warming up and cooling down before and after each exercise period are important factors to avoid muscle strain.*

SKIN – Wrinkles & Sagging

Skin changes are among the most visible signs of aging, with several changes related to sun exposure, calling for lifelong prevention

- Outer skin layer thins as the number of cells holding pigment decreases, resulting in aging skin appearing thinner, paler, translucent, especially in Caucasians

- The top fat layer thins resulting in a reduced ability to maintain body temperature

- Sagging skin (turkey neck, arm bat wings) and a loss of skin resilience due to the top fat layer thinning

- Age spots, sometimes called liver spots, are harmless large pigmented areas that have been exposed over many years to the sun

- Wrinkles and leathery weather-beaten looks are due to connective tissue changes that reduce the skin's elasticity

- Blood vessels in the dermis layer become fragile, leading to easy bruising and capillary bleeding under the skin

- Wound healing is four times slower

- Oil production reduces (in men after age 80, in women after menopause) causing dry, itchy skin that has lost its moistness

- Less sweat is produced leading to the risk of overheating and heatstroke

- Skin growths, rough patches, skin blemishes – some kind of skin disorder are common in 90% of older people

- Skin sensitivities result from the top layer of dermis fat thinning bringing nerve endings closer to the surface

Gentle Aging Healthy Idea*: wear sunscreen year-round, wear sun protective clothing, maintain a good diet, take vitamins, drink plenty of fluids, moisturize liberally daily and especially generously after a hot bath.*

Eliminate stress which contributes to even slower surface wound healing.

HAIR

Whitening or graying of the hair, can begin happening in the 30s, starting at the temples.

- Aging hair follicles produce less pigment (melanin).

- Body and facial hair turn gray later than scalp hair

- Graying is genetically determined, earlier for Caucasians, later for Asians

- 25% of men start balding by age 30; two thirds of men have significant baldness by age 60

- Females lose hair density all over as they age. Body and facial hair (on chin, around the lips) that remain becomes coarse.

- Male eyebrows, ears, nose hair becomes long and coarse

Gentle Aging Health Idea: *dyeing one's hair is one control that everyone can do to stave off the visual appearance of aging for as long as desirable. Aging with gray highlights is a natural way to accept the inevitable at a certain age.*

NAILS

Nails thicken, ridge, split

- With aging, nail growth slows

- Nails can become brittle and dull

- Nails can become yellow and opaque

- Fingernail tips may fragment

- Toenails may become hard and thick

- Ingrown toenails are more of a problem

- Lengthwise ridges can develop

- Medical conditions (diabetes, limited circulation) can exacerbate age related

Gentle Aging Healthy Idea*: do not neglect nail care, especially toenail grooming, which can affect walking ability and comfort. Reduced flexibility can make toenail grooming difficult to self-perform. Wear footwear with plenty of toe space.*

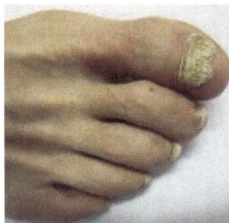

HABITS Entrench

With aging, quirky tendencies intensify as comfortable habits settle in; mental attitude change comes very slowly, if change happens at all

- Filters and inhibitions are lost

- Old meanness can surface, resulting in demanding behavior

- Lose willingness for spur-of-the-moment spontaneity

Gentle Aging Healthy Idea: *continue to keep the brain agile and sharp by enjoying mental challenges like crossword puzzles, learning new things, reading, taking courses, engaging in philosophical deep discussions. A flexible mind doesn't need to age or diminish with time.*

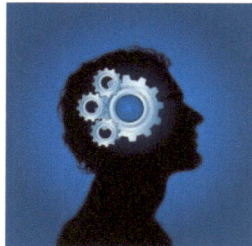

MEMORY

"Senior moments" are wrongly named for memory slips, as the aging mind in the senior years is just as sharp, or sharper, than ever.

- We think we lose brain function as we age, but the opposite is true: the brain is 'plastic' – it can remake itself, with an endless supply of neural connections to call upon.

- The brain shrinks and brain cells die every day, but there are so many billions available that they can never all be used and everyone can easily spare those thousands of cells that die off daily.

- The brain is like a muscle – it must be exercised and used to develop strength

Gentle Healthy Aging Idea: *using the brain in old age, when we have more time, is a great way to exercise it with new learnings, helping higher level thinking improve at any age. Use it or lose it!*

*NOTE: For a much fuller treatment on Memory, see the SmartyPants Secrets book MEMORY, at www.SmartyPantsSecrets.com/books

Changes in Other Senses – Taste, Smell, Touch

Taste and smell are importantly intertwined in the enjoyment of food; smell for safety of detecting dangerous gases, smoke, food rot.

- The number of taste buds decrease with age; remaining taste buds lose some ability, requiring more and more (i.e. salt) to taste

- Less saliva is produced, affecting taste. Gums recede, bones and teeth soften, requiring softer foods

- Smell begins to decrease early, in males in their late 20s, in females in their early 30s.

- As the 5 taste buds are reduced, sweet is the last one to go, leaving many seniors with an outsized sweet tooth

- Changes in touch sensitivity - ability to feel vibration, pressure, temperature, and pain

- Health issues and medication treatments can impact the reduced ability/loss of different senses

Gentle Healthy Aging Idea: *taking extra care around hot and cold areas to prevent skin damage (burns, frostbite)*

Women Outlive Men

The US life expectancy has women living 4.8 years on average longer than men, with real time results of 5-10 years that women outlive men in the industrialized world. Of all people over 100 years old, 85% are female. Even in the animal kingdom, females outlive males. Why is this the case?

The answer from Mother Nature is simple: women are needed longer to nurture and care for young offspring, so they are built sturdier than men, who are only needed in conception and are technically disposable afterwards. Hence women have 2 X chromosomes, a complete duplicate backup set of genes to draw on for cell generation; men have only one X chromosome, so no choice if a gene is faulty.

The #1 cause of death for both genders is heart disease, with men predisposed to developing cardiovascular problems about 10 years before women. This is attributable to menses; women are physiologically protected from heart disease in a number of ways over men until menopause.

But as 70% of longevity is environment (versus genetic) and we know that heart disease is a huge obstacle, there is much that both genders can do to mitigate the chance of getting heart disease, mainly avoiding known contributing factors of:

- Smoking

- Diet – high cholesterol foods, red meat

- Lack of exercise

- Stress

On the last one, stress, women have a big advantage with the quality of their stronger social networks. Men may pal around with their guy friends, but they tend to hold on to their worries and stress; women reach out and talk to others with their problematic issues (thank you, oxytocin, the 'bonding' female hormone that promotes interactive nurturing behavior, useful in raising children). Married men benefit from this concept and are proven to live longer due to female companionship.

The older you get in good health, the more you can compress the sick years until the end. Getting older and sicker needs to be reframed as the older you get, the healthier you've been.

How to LOOK, feel, and think 10 years younger

There used to be a TV show called "10 Years Younger" where applicants put into a glass box in a public square, and strangers were asked to guess their age. Then they were enhanced without invasive procedures, and re-staged for public guessing. The before and after answers were tallied and resulted in most people guessing at least 10 years younger after the makeovers.

The net result of the show was that people primarily guess a person's youthfulness based on:

- Hair (color not gray, stylish cut, bounce, shine)

- Dress (well fitted to camouflage problems, stylish, proper colors)

- Energy (movement in the box, smile!)

- Females: Makeup (accenting positive features, covering up blemishes)

Since everyone self-selected wants to 'win' and look younger, and everyone enjoys new clothes, a new haircut, and positive attention, the show producers had an easy time of it.

We too can do the same thing with similar results. Additionally, to look and feel younger, add to the list:

- Drink lots of water! – drink more water, not less, as bodily fluids need to be maintained, to keep skin plump, eyes moist, saliva flowing, blood building, etc.

- Do Kegel exercises! - habitually strengthening the lower muscles can stave off incontinence (wearing diapers will surely make you feel old!)

- Do mental challenges! – keep the brain sharp with daily jumbles, soduko, crosswords, figuring out mysteries, mental math calculations, logic puzzles.

- Makeover your smile by whitening your teeth! Use white strips to improve the appearance of teeth, a big aging cue

- Put a spring in your step! Gait is the #1 way we determine a person's age. The energy of a youthful mind can be reflected in energetic lively movement. Stay active.

- Floss! Gums are indicative of underlying health; flossing 'adds' 6 years to life.

What Age Are YOU 'Frozen' At Mentally?

I have asked several in my cohort this question of late: what age are you still, in your head?

When we have a calendar birthday, it's really just another day... which turns into another week, another month, another year... And so the years pass along, but we don't notice the changes mentally, since we don't really know what we're supposed to be like at any age. And is 20 really so different from 30? Certainly no difference mentally.

We still think the same, with a bit more wisdom and experience as we age, but that's only if we give them some good thought and learn from life's myriad experiences. The same could be said mentally of a toddler from a middle-schooler, with the big difference in physical ability during the developmental years, and the accompanying independence.

But with adults that are at peak physical development and fully independent, do you really change much in mental age in your mind? Do you view yourself much differently over the decades?

When I posed the question, the common

answer for people in their early 60s was 30-35. Most people feel that they were at their best in their early 30s and so remain mentally at their peak for several decades, never aging beyond. That's good – continue to think young, and you'll resist succumbing to the self-talk limitation of "*I can't do that at MY age"*.

I also asked my 90 year old uncle what age he was in his head, and he said 70. But he was a youthful 70, still trying new things. So with advanced age comes the realization that you really aren't 35 any longer.

For my part, I truly froze at 18 years old – I still think I can do anything, still have the impetuousness of youth, and some of the foolhardiness also. I wish the same for all of you like-minded others ☺

Remember that age is only in your own mind - you are truly as young (and as old) as you think.

A Word on Immortality

No matter what they claim, no one truly wants to live forever, to outlive your family and friends would be more curse than fun. But we do want to continue to contribute as long as we are healthy and able.

To gain realistic longevity, human 'immortality', pay attention to

- *family* (close relationships are a proven lifeline)

- *health* (don't put off seeking medical help, as a long life of pain is not a good life)

- being *less egotistical* (admit it, it's really not all about you!)

and you will live a good life, even long after you're gone ☺

The SmartyPants Secret on AGING:

Keep Moving - don't stop doing things; resist telling yourself that you're too old to do such and such any longer. Instead adjust the extent and the speed that you do things in accordance with your older diminished abilities, but keep on keeping on, maintain your physical and mental flexibility.

As the body stiffens with age, the mind-body connection then tends to also stiffen the mind, needlessly losing the mental flexibility to be spontaneous.

While the body is a machine that likes regular routine, the mind is the opposite, thriving on the challenge of learning and doing new things, stretching in new ways, creating new neural connections.

BOOK BUYER BONUS

As a thank you to buyers, there is an additional free resource available only to book buyers. Did you get yours? If you missed it, go to www.SmartyPantsSecrets.com/bookbonus .

It's has additional valuable content and is free to book buyers, so don't miss out on getting yours!

ABOUT

I am DR Martin, PhD* (*Personal human Development expertise) – Dolley Rapoport Martin. I took Dolley as my first name* in honor of the great First Lady Dolley Madison, whom I admire for her heroic actions in the White House during very turbulent times.

I took Rapoport as a middle name* in honor of Ingeborg Rapoport, who at age 103, is the oldest person to be awarded a Doctorate; finally getting the recognition due her from 77 years prior in Nazi Germany, unfairly denied her due to her Jewish roots. There is so much injustice in the world; it is an honor to recognize her achievement by taking her name. [*The selecting of one's name is an important exercise, since names are so personal and tied to identity. Yet most of us go through life with a name not of our choosing. Check out the SmartyPants Secret book NAMES.]

I have studied every communication subject for more than a decade, acquiring a large body of knowledge. I, perhaps like you, am a voracious reader and learner. My other strength is that I retain much of what I learn, so I can then compile the knowledge on a variety of subjects into a concise format, making the books that I author a shortcut on the best knowledge available. This saves you from going through all the data looking for the kernel that makes the greatest difference in success, the SmartyPants secret on a given topic.

I also have a mind that is ever curious about so many topics. I have earned multiple expert designations (education certified English teacher, Real Estate Broker, Stock Broker series 7, series 6, series, Certified Financial Manager, Insurance producer certified, Coach University) and held high level positions in business – large corporate entities, privately held companies, non-profit organizations, and startups – and have volunteered extensively, holding executive positions at the local, district and national levels. So I've been around the block more than once, on more than one topic.

Due to my research and experience, I have logged the perquisite time to carry the title of expert, giving myself an honorary PhD in the expertise area of communication, Personal human Development. I am passionate about sharing the knowledge that I have gained with you, in bite-size pieces.

And when a certain topic is not in my field of expertise, I find an expert with deep expertise in the field who has the knowledge that I seek. I then ask numerous in-depth questions of the expert to get to the gist, learn the SmartyPants Secret, to then pass the knowledge on in a book on the subject.

For other titles and additional resources, visit www.SmartyPantsSecrets.com

All book titles at www.amazon.com/-/e/B018HA35I8

Watch for content clips and helpful technique tips on a variety of topics coming soon at www.youtube.com/c/smartypantssecrets

Contact: Info@SmartyPantsSecrets.com